BE
THE
CHANGE
(maker)

LESSONS FROM THOSE WHO ARE &
A CATALYST FOR THOSE WHO WILL

Kara Exner

KARA EXNER

◆ FriesenPress

Suite 300 - 990 Fort St
Victoria, BC, V8V 3K2
Canada

www.friesenpress.com

Author Photograph: © Lori Maloney

ISBN
978-1-5255-6262-4 (Hardcover)
978-1-5255-6263-1 (Paperback)
978-1-5255-6264-8 (eBook)

1. BUSINESS & ECONOMICS, NONPROFIT ORGANIZATIONS & CHARITIES

Distributed to the trade by The Ingram Book Company

Dedicated to my husband and our two boys:
You are consistent role models for how to
make a difference, and you patiently
forgive me when I'm not.

CONTENTS

MY PASSION
FOR THIS PROJECT

"**D**o you see yourself as a changemaker?"

The question was direct, from someone I trust. I had really hoped I wouldn't cry during this gathering of wise and trusted allies, but that was a tall order—so passionate am I for this project.

"I don't know," I managed to whisper as tears welled. Then I pulled it together and looked within. "Sometimes, at work, I feel like I'm making a difference. Like last week, I think I made a difference."

"Isn't that enough?" he asked.

Crap, these questions were hard. Wanting to make a difference may be a calling, but that undertaking still must meet, and then come through, our humanness—via all the emotions that reside within.

For me, the undertaking has been nine years in the making, and my emotions have spanned the continuum. I was both euphoric and relieved to finally figure out that my purpose is to help everyday people become successful changemakers. I was energized and simply delighted to satisfy my curiosity by asking changemakers how they did it. I have been frustrated by my inability to move the project forward faster. I have felt dejected after some rejection, and fear has ducked in and out along the way, almost always when I'm about to step into the unknown with a presentation, or when working on this book.

I have learned firsthand that changemaking is not for the faint of heart. And yet, when asked if it's not enough to feel like I sometimes make a difference in my day job, I answered, "This is what I know: pursuing this, the changemaker project . . . this is the real stuff. This is my true calling, and I want to do more of it."

INTRODUCTION

Do you want to change the world? Are you looking for more ways to make a positive difference? Is doing good, and making things better, part of your personal values and beliefs? If so, may you be as compelled to read this book as I was to write it.

Many of us drawn to make a difference in our workplace or community find leaders like Nelson Mandela or Mother Teresa to be intimidating role models, or difficult to relate to. While there's no question these icons are positioned to have incredible impact, there are ordinary, everyday people all around us who are successfully changing the world by focusing on their piece of it.

In my mission to help more people make a positive difference, I endeavoured to learn about changemakers, to see what they have in common, then record my findings so that the ways of the changemakers—those who make the world a better place—can be known to all.

Changemakers are usually humble people, doers who generally wish no personal fanfare. Though the Conclusion provides information on the types of people I interviewed, those same individuals would advise, as do I, to focus on their message.

And that is what you will find forms the bulk of this book: genuine advice delivered from actual changemakers. They have practices, beliefs, and mindsets in common with each other. For them, changemaking is how they approach life. And the great thing is, the approach can be learned.

The people I interviewed aren't famous in the way our culture defines celebrity. So, while you may not 'know of' the interviewees, you may be familiar with equally dedicated teachers in your own life, with volunteers in your community who never seem to tire of giving their time and talents, or with a friend you know who works in a non-profit agency for little pay, but who claims other, less tangible rewards.

What brings new changemakers to the stage—or closer to it? Learning that most changemakers are everyday folks. It's more relatable and less intimidating to read about people who are recognizable in a 'has peanut butter on toast' kind of way.

The research findings—or what I discovered—are grouped into three sections:

1. How changemakers perceive themselves.
2. How changemakers relate to others.
3. How changemakers orient themselves to action.

Each section contains a number of themes, with the changemakers' own words written in italics. So, whether you prefer to read in order, or roam here and there, I encourage you to start where you want and see what resonates. Be sure, though, to take some time with the reflective questions sprinkled throughout. Make this your changemaker handbook: ask your own questions, jot some notes, and after each section, write or doodle what you most want to remember from that section. Do this to learn how the themes are alive in you, and to activate the next steps on your changemaker path.

Look around: our world needs you more than ever.

Section 1

HOW CHANGEMAKERS PERCEIVE THEMSELVES

It's rarely easy to tell the truth about ourselves: our real emotions, our true goals, when we're not fulfilling our potential, and when and where we get in our own way. While not easy, changemakers tell the truth anyway, confidently and without apology. They have learned the benefits of being honest about who they are. None of those I interviewed claimed to have it all figured out, but their heightened sense of self-awareness, and their ability to discuss it, was refreshing and sophisticated.

STRENGTHS AND WEAKNESSES

It became clear early in the research that changemakers speak openly about both their strengths and their weaknesses. This was apparent in *what* they talked about, and also in *how* they talked about it: their immediate responses, their lack of hesitation when sharing the hard truths about themselves, and their ability to speak strongly about their strengths without needing to apologize or downplay them. These were all clues that these folks own what they're good at, that they know what they're not good at, and that they have no problem saying so with sureness.

Have you noticed that many people feel they are boasting or arrogant if they speak about their strengths? Perhaps this comes from how many of us have been raised to be humble and to not 'toot our own horns.' No matter where it comes from, it seems people equate confidence with conceit. Changemakers are simply confident. Being clear on their strengths means:

- knowing where they prefer to use their energy, what tasks *give* them energy, what lifts them up, and what drains them or drags them down;
- finding ways to use their strengths as often as possible, and delegate to others the areas where they're not as strong (refer to Ask for Help and Collaborate within Section 2 to learn more); and
- continuing to build and refine their strengths to become their most effective.

"When it comes to change, I like to use the word 'improvement.' I see myself at the front of the pack, arm waving, and being a champion for those improvements. I tend to focus on the 'what' and then other people who are better suited can translate the arm waving into processes and procedures, and in so doing, define the 'how.'"

Do you know anyone who is reluctant to disclose their weaknesses? I've worked with many people who feel speaking openly about their weaknesses would make them vulnerable, or put them at a disadvantage.

Changemakers, on the other hand, speak openly and confidently about their weaknesses. For some of them, this is the key to identifying what they need to get help with. They are highly self-aware individuals. This theme about knowing oneself goes beyond lists of strengths and weaknesses. It also includes:

- being willing to find out what you don't know;
- knowing your values, biases, and assumptions, and how you respond in different situations and to different types of people;
- knowing your limitations and expectations;
- admitting mistakes;
- letting go of the ego;
- knowing your criteria for finding happiness in your work; and
- making distinctions between what you're good at and what is your passion and purpose.

Self-awareness also emerged in response to a specific question about the biggest obstacle changemakers have faced. While a number of external barriers were reported, almost all changemakers disclosed that they themselves are the biggest obstacle. For example, they spoke about:

- personal beliefs that don't serve them;
- the negative effects when they compare themselves to others;
- the difficulty in discerning between an intuitive nudge and true fear;
- unhelpful inner dialogue;
- holding on too tightly to their own position;
- an unwillingness to engage in self-promotion; and
- needing to think differently about themselves, or redefining who they thought they were.

No matter the specific self-barrier, changemakers' willingness to admit that they are their own toughest obstacles is one of their biggest strengths, for it is through this awareness that they are able to make different choices in order to overcome what stops or hinders them.

I'm a fan and student of the emerging field of positive psychology. When I took my psychology degree in the early 1990's, there wasn't much positivity associated with the field. The focus seemed to be on problematic conditions and dysfunctional personalities. When I first heard about positive psychology in 2008, I was instantly compelled to learn more about this field which studies the more positive aspects of being human, such as character strengths, quality relationships, meaning, and happiness. While I am grateful for psychology's focus on how to help those with depression, anxiety, and other mental illnesses, I am also grateful for what positive psychology research is teaching us about how to thrive.

One of the most common ways people resist the messages of positive psychology is they think it means we only look at the good stuff, and that we should avoid acknowledging risks, threats, or negativity. This is not at all what the field of positive psychology advocates. Just ask my mentor and colleague Robert Biswas-Diener (a positive psychology researcher and a changemaker interviewee), who co-authored a book entitled *The Upside of Your Dark Side: Why Being Your Whole Self—Not Just Your "Good" Self—Drives Success and Fulfillment* (Kashdan & Biswas-Diener, 2014). Positive psychology endeavours to help us recognize that our world is—that *we* are—comprised of positive and negative aspects. Changemakers know this; it's a key part of their mindsets.

It was from Robert Biswas-Diener that I learned the best way to reconcile strengths and weaknesses. His sailboat metaphor has stayed with me over the years, and others have found it valuable, too. He has written about the metaphor (Biswas-Diener, 2010, p. 31), and I heard him speak about it at a conference in this way:

> The sails on a sailboat are your strengths. They help get you where you want and need to go. The hull of the boat is sometimes where leaks appear. These are your weaknesses. If you spring a small crack or leak that doesn't let on very much water, then who cares? These small cracks or weaknesses will not hinder you; your sails—your strengths—can still get you where you need to go. But if the hole in the boat gets bigger, and it *is* letting on more water such that it could impede you or sink you, then you need to repair this weakness. So we take our boat into dry-dock to repair the leak. But notice what sometimes happens: we spend so much time patching and fixing so that no water will ever get in again, that we miss out on going anywhere. So at some point we need to get back in the water and unfurl our sails—our strengths—and let them take us forward. (R. Biswas-Diener, personal communication, October 30, 2010)

As Robert says, "Focusing on only strengths or only on weaknesses is not sufficient" (Biswas-Diener, 2010, p. 31).

Your turn:

What do you believe are your strengths?

What would others say are your strengths?

How can you use more of your strengths to achieve your goals?

What would others say is a weakness in you?

What would YOU say is a weakness for you—that others wouldn't guess?

What benefits could you (or do you already) gain from being more confident about your strengths and more honest about your weaknesses?

BALANCE AND BOUNDARIES

In addition to knowing their strengths and weaknesses, changemakers are also acutely aware of the structures and habits that help them be effective. They look after their physical, mental, emotional, and spiritual health—not always perfectly, and not 100% of the time, but making space for self-care is a priority, no matter how committed they are to their cause.

The changemakers spoke about the importance of creating boundaries and finding balance. They are intentional about where they choose to spend their time, and also how they choose to expend their energy. Recently, I have noticed more interest in the idea of energy management over time management. It's not just about how we effectively use the hours and minutes in our day, but how we align our energy with our tasks to be most productive. For example, Pat Katz, an expert on issues of balance, stress, wellness, and productivity, has written about the importance of building buffer time after returning from travel or after completing a large project (Katz, 2013). It's a way to look after oneself, and look after the things that might've been missed, instead of booking in another large commitment or project immediately.

My own version of this is recognizing that, while something may 'look good on paper' (read: there is space for it in the schedule), it will be too stressful to jam too many things into that space. For example, I know I won't be able to enjoy the family vacation if I'm booked to deliver a workshop the day after returning. Instead, I'll reserve a few days for returning calls, catching up on email, and doing final workshop preparations, as well as tending to the more mundane household tasks like unpacking, doing laundry, and getting groceries. It's not glamorous, but it's what works to help me stay present and relaxed to enjoy the vacation time with my family.

Changemakers know this and they employ several strategies to ensure they are looking after themselves and their energy:

- They **don't over-commit,** and they often have a litmus test for how they decide if they will say yes to a request.

  "If your first instinct is to say yes, then build in safety nets; have systems in place to give yourself time to think it over. We are so inclined to say yes, and may regret that later."

  "Anything I do has to meet two criteria: Is it giving back to my community? And, do I want to do it? If one of those goes off sync, it's a reminder to me: I may be contributing, but I don't want to do it. I try not to get carried away by ego, but go back to those questions. If I embark on something, and it's not right, I have the nerve and energy to pull away from it."

- They **look for work-life flexibility**, not necessarily work-life balance.

- They **take time to clear their minds**, because they know that their brains work better when not under pressure. Meditation, walking, running, CrossFit, prayer, writing, and mindfulness exercises are all ways changemakers clear their heads.

"I do my best thinking when I'm alone and walking— you have to be very comfortable with yourself. I have made a habit of building into my day some pull-away time. Some time when it's just thoughtful, or I'm not even concretely thinking, but the answers will come."

"Sometimes when having difficulty finding a solution to a challenging problem, it may be better to set it aside—change your focus or take a break from work. Your sub-conscious mind will continue to work at it and a solution may emerge more easily than if you doggedly try to force it."

- They **keep something in reserve**. Whether it's money or energy or emotional strength, change-makers keep a reserve 'in the bank.' They go at their goals with gusto, and they also ensure they have support. They avoid extremes, and they don't put all their eggs in one basket.

"Don't put the demand that your game-changing thing must be the provider for your life. I live in Hollywood and people do it all the time. Don't put the demand on

it to provide an income for you. It may provide for you, but don't demand it."

"Emotionally, financially, you need to keep something in reserve for another challenge; if you're extended in personal resources, you'll miss opportunities that are low hanging fruit. Never be going 100% flat out in personal or financial resources. I guess it comes from growing up in Saskatchewan, where you're always ready for the next bump."

Overall, changemakers simply make time to develop and practise good habits. From starting each morning with a mission, to ensuring they have structure when working from home or alone, these folks are intentional in how they create an approach that works for *them*, not just for their cause.

Your turn:

What does balance mean to you?

What do you find most difficult to say "no" to?

What is your own litmus test of criteria before you'll say "yes" to something?

How can you tell when you're off balance?

What two small actions would have the greatest impact on your ability to practise balance more consistently?

BE CURIOUS AND KEEP LEARNING

The changemakers I interviewed are all smart, experienced, and resourceful. Many of them have completed doctoral level studies, and many are considered leading experts in their fields. Even so, no matter their background or their current area of focus, almost all of them spoke about the critical importance of never stopping learning. The value of nearly every form of education was reported: continuing education, personal development, formal training, professional upgrading, and learning from experience.

There are fascinating layers here: it is about on-going learning and development, but it's also about curiosity, humility, and the ability to shut up and listen.

Many changemakers linked learning to curiosity. They are curious about other people, they are curious about other ways of life, and they are curious about themselves. They understand the value of asking lots of questions, and they are keen to seek opinions and advice from different sources.

Changemakers see failures, setbacks, obstacles, and naysayers as opportunities for learning. For example, when I asked specifically what they would've done differently, almost all changemakers responded with some version of "everything has led me to this point . . . yes, there have been mistakes or setbacks, but you learn from it all and move forward . . . look at it as an opportunity to re-evaluate and try again . . . take the good from the situation and grow from it."

"I'm not afraid to fail. I don't like it, but I accept small failures and setbacks. It's inevitable. I'm okay with small failures as learning experiences."

"Every single step of the way, it's been a step up. Where we are right now is one of the pinnacles, I feel, and we've gotten here because of where we've been. There have been small things that have been fine-tuned. But they are just little things. I try not to look at anything as if I've failed, I look at it truly as an opportunity. Let's look at this, let's re-evaluate, and step again."

Being open-minded and maintaining humility are essential for learning. Changemakers can see the positive impact they're having—even celebrate it—without being pretentious about it. While they are confident, they are not arrogant. More often than not, changemakers know—and admit—they don't know it all. This perspective is also linked to the theme of knowing one's weaknesses. They have the humility to admit when they've made mistakes, acknowledge when others have something of value to offer, and openly commit, enroll, or sign-up to learn more.

"Surround yourself with people who are as good as or better than you. I took this advice from a film-maker friend. He loves to be the dumbest person in the room. That's when he learns the most."

It's not enough only to be curious and ask questions. You also need to listen. I have been teaching a Listen with Presence module in my Coaching Skills for Leaders courses for ten years. One of the questions I almost always ask is, "What is the impact when we listen attentively? It could be the impact on you, on the other person, or on the relationship." In addition to all the answers you might expect about increased trust, people feeling validated, and deeper connections, I often hear that you can learn A LOT when you listen really well, including new information, fresh perspectives, and a richer understanding of others. Changemakers know this, too.

"We have two ears and one mouth for a reason; we should use them in that ratio. Not listening and not actively listening is a path to trouble. Don't fall into the trap that your way is the only way or your opinion is the only valid one."

"Be humble and listen."

Your turn:

If you could learn more about anything, what would you pursue, and how would you find out about it?

What un-learnings might you need to consider in order to create space for new learning to take place?

What kinds of things do you get curious about?

How has learning from experience shifted your mindset?

What are some of the lessons you've learned through failure?

SEEK ALIGNMENT

Overwhelmingly, changemakers reported the importance of staying true to one's values, following one's passion, and staying focused on one's vision. The data from the interviews is plentiful for these elements of values, passion, and vision. It wasn't initially clear how these concepts fit together until a further review of the data revealed another word: Alignment.

Changemakers are strong advocates that this work of leading positive change ought to be aligned with what is important to them.

VALUES

Our values are at the core of who we are. They are what we believe in, what is important to us, and what helps us choose among different paths. Our values aren't found in a book or learned in a course, but they can be revealed to us. We can become aware of what we value and tap into what already exists within us. Changemakers used many different words and phrases to describe how they define values, and the importance of those values:

Staying true to yourself: This means knowing your own reasons for pursuing your work, and remaining committed to them, even in the face of conflicting opinions. It means standing your ground and being okay with being out there alone.

Doing what you love: This includes valuing *what* you do as well as valuing *how you feel about* what you do. It can range from being aware of what you like and noticing opportunities to do the work you like, to looking around for what excites you and not walking away from it. It can also mean doing what's fun, what makes you happy, and what you find interesting.

Aligning with what's important: Ensuring your work is aligned with your values, beliefs, and principles—making decisions based on how things feel and fit with your value system.

PASSION

Author Elizabeth Gilbert wrote an interesting post about not living someone else's dream (Gilbert, 2014). She wrote that, after the success of her book *Eat Pray Love*, she could've had her own television show, could've stayed in Rome or Bali, could've hired staff to help her grow her brand, and so on, but she didn't do any of those things because they were somebody else's dream—or somebody else's dream for her:

> I was thinking today about all the other paths that I did not take in life, no matter how shiny and appealing they may have looked. I've had the possibility of living so many different kinds of life that could have been a dream for somebody else. I never chose those lives. I've never lived the dreams that other people

wanted for themselves—nor have I lived the dreams that other people may have wanted for me. (Gilbert, 2014, para. 4)

Instead of pursuing what is "shiny and appealing," Ms. Gilbert's litmus test is to ask herself, *What makes me come to life?*

I know what makes me come to life—working on my books . . . Knowing what makes me come to life has helped me to distinguish between my dreams and the dreams of others.

WHAT MAKES YOU COME TO LIFE?

Ask yourself this question whenever you are given any choice or opportunity. Ask: "Will saying YES to this path bring me closer to the source that brings me to life? Or will it take me further away?"

No matter how alluring, no matter how beautiful, no matter how sparkling and fancy and delicious—do not say YES to other people's dreams.

Do your own thing. Live in your own waking dream. Stubbornly. (Gilbert, 2014, para. 12-16)

What makes us come to life is a great way to view passion. Where values are akin to our core, passion is the fuel that helps us do the work. While many changemakers used the word "passion" to describe what they do (they are passionate), and in response to a question regarding the advice they'd give others (be passionate), there were a variety of ways they spoke about it:

Passion for the cause, not desire to make change. Many changemakers spoke about the power of doing this work for the right reasons: doing something for good, not just for the sake of change; having passion for the cause or initiative itself versus wanting to change something; focusing on a client's growth, or the positive impact on a client group, and not on change. In other words, successful changemakers aren't motivated by changing the world; they are motivated to make a positive difference for the cause they really care about.

"You have to realize change happens slowly. You are not necessarily embarking on change; it's about identifying a place to start. Sometimes you have to start very, very slowly and work at changing attitudes and work by example. . . . Rather than thinking you have to change the world, you think about what is my part in creating a system that is responsible for the well-being of youth? What is my part in this change?"

Sometimes passion comes from negative emotions. Changemakers readily admit that it's sometimes the seemingly negative emotions that motivate them. Whether they describe it as being motivated by encountering challenges, being thirsty or hungry to fulfill a mission, or not being afraid of anger and injustice because those things can actually be fuel, changemakers see the value of getting riled up.

"I take my stress and fears and use them as a driving force to help people. You can learn a lot from the things that upset you. You can draw from that, and use it to help others and

help yourself. You use it as rocket fuel (propellant)—even though it's explosive and harmful, it will move you forward versus into the quicksand of despair. That's what I do, and it makes me feel good."

Sometimes passion is spoken about as love. Changemakers often use the word "love" to describe how they feel about the work they do:

"If your motivation is out of love for others or the planet, you can't go wrong."

"I love my clients."

"I do what I love."

Author and trainer Rick Tamlyn wrote an article about how—when asked about the work we do—we tend to respond by talking about the business we're in. Another option when answering the question about our work is to talk about the business we're *really* in (Tamlyn, 2018). His own answer to that question is another example of how our love for our passion is motivating:

> I am a trainer, keynoter, author, executive coach, and team development leader, which are all great answers when the world needs a simple answer to what I do. Yet the business I am really in is "to make your Bigger Game real." I just love saying that! It

compels me, it creates me and it gets me out of bed fast (most mornings!).

So I ask you, "What business are you REALLY in?" (Tamlyn, 2018, para. 10-11)

Passion engages others. Sometimes passion looks like a loud rallying cry, and sometimes it looks like quiet tenacity. Either way, changemakers agree that when other people see your passion—see you speaking from a place of passion—it excites and engages them.

"When you connect to the deeper meaning of what you are doing, and have more longevity, people will want to be part of it."

In fact, when you allow your passion to shine, it enables others to be true to themselves, too.

"As a kid, I learned to 'dim' myself, to stay safe. As I get older, I'm learning to 'un-dim' myself, to be really conscious. . . . The more I share who I am at a soul level, the more satisfying it is. And by bringing even deeper layers of myself out, it gives other people permission to do the same."

Passion can mean you'll be on your own. A number of changemakers acknowledged that following their passion means they're not doing what everyone else is doing but, instead, charting their own path. All who spoke about passion and charting one's own path agreed that it's not only worth it, it's essential, and it links to being aligned with what is important to YOU.

Sometimes, passion won't let go of you. Some changemakers were able to articulate the feeling of being inhabited by a definite pull or call to do this work. They feel they "need" to do it even though there may be big obstacles, or that it's addictive and it feels odd if they're not doing it. Some also talked about getting "hints and clues from the universe that they cannot ignore," and that it "gets into their brain and they can't get it out."

"It's like Hotel California—you can check out anytime, but you can never leave."

Your turn:

What makes you come to life?

What values have you revealed that you can't live without?

What causes are you passionate about?

What angers or riles you enough to take action?

What do you love to do?

What is so important that you'll pursue it, even if you're the only one?

GETTING STARTED

How changemakers got started was different for each—it was not something common across the board. Some leadership books talk about defining moments when one's purpose becomes clear or the goal is illuminated. I didn't ask about this in the interviews, and a clear theme did not emerge in this regard in response to my other questions.

Initially, I felt sheepish about this, like it was an obvious theme that I somehow missed. But the diverse ways in which changemakers came to get started can be positive, for they illustrate that there is no one, right way to begin making a difference in the world. How people find their way to the changemaker path is varied, and the diversity of examples may help you see yourself on the path, or getting closer to it.

Seeing a need that exists can be the first step. One of the most common ways changemakers got started was seeing a need that existed or a gap where something was missing, and then finding a solution. For some changemakers it was recognizing the same challenges of others as they had experienced themselves. For others it was stepping back from their current environment to gain perspective and learn new things, and then stepping back in to help fix it.

"The system is broken and it needs to be fixed. Complex problems require multi-faceted solutions and I created a solution to help fix a complex problem."

"The motivation comes from a place of activism and advocacy, where I recognize something that's missing, I recognize a possible solution, and I accept that a lot of hours and a lot of hard work will be involved. There's a possibility to create a solution to address that need in society."

"The motivation came from my own personal struggle . . . and realizing how many others were struggling with it, too. So, noticing that I wasn't alone, I could channel the struggle. Had everything come easy to me, I don't know I'd be in this place. The struggle opened my eyes to what needed to change, what is lacking out there."

Personal dissatisfaction can be the catalyst. Being frustrated, unhappy, and/or fed up with their current situation was enough for many changemakers to quit a job, leave a relationship, or shift their business focus, in order to find or create more meaningful work and a more meaningful life. Examples include: being unfulfilled working in the corporate sector; having had enough of being an employee; feeling bored and deciding to take stock of the current situation; feeling tired of what they had been doing for a long time; being frustrated by ongoing obstacles; and, one of my favourites, knowing they could do more.

"I got tired of what I was doing. I looked at my life and asked myself if I should keep doing what I'm doing or do something that makes people feel good. I quit my job and have been doing this for four years."

Changemakers admit this is not an easy route. There are a lot of unknowns when you contemplate leaving behind what is familiar ('better the devil you know than the devil you don't' type of idea), but, eventually, the pain of not doing it outweighed the pain of the fears, and they made their move.

"You've got to be sick and tired of where you're at. You've got to have a big enough 'why'—a big enough target—that something is burning and is deep enough that it compels you to act in spite of your habits."

"The pain of staying at my job was greater than losing what I had. That was the breaking point; I got creative."

Sometimes there is no clear plan. Some changemakers reported they simply got caught up in the effort and that there wasn't a plan or a goal in mind. Some folks fell into it, others fell into it but made a conscious decision to *stay* in it. Some changemakers just started and found that ideas and processes became clearer as they went along. Others got started and then stuck with it until their idea evolved and they got traction. Following one's curiosity is another method, as is the belief that everything happens for a reason, but sometimes you have to go looking for the reason.

Some changemakers are influenced at an early age. Growing up in a family culture where volunteering is the norm, and where parents set an example of giving back to one's community, can be impactful. Some changemakers were motivated to follow their parents' example. This influenced them to want to make a difference.

For other changemakers, the childhood influence was not a positive one.

For example, many middle-aged women spoke about the limitations put on them by their parents or other adults in their lives. For them, restricted belief systems held by others about what they should—and should not—pursue was a barrier to the women's aspirations to be out in the world making a difference. Breaking free of these constraints and pre-determined roles was challenging.

And still, for another group, childhood hardships and adversity had an impact on shaping their desire to make a difference.

"It goes back to my childhood as a refugee from the Nazis—when you see injustice and violence, you ask questions about whether it has to be that way. Right/left, western/ eastern—there are no answers to what kind of social structures are needed. Our human capacities for compassion are what's needed."

"When I went through school I was the youngest, I was picked last, and I developed an 'I'll show you' attitude."

Personal values can set the direction. The values, beliefs, principles, and personal mantras that the changemakers articulated were as diverse as the changemakers themselves. Some folks talked about how—as humans—we should all be making a difference, or that we all have a role to play as citizens. Others spoke about legacy; some talked about leading by example; others referred to the future and the impact we can make.

"I feel I am a tool in the hands of God. I serve."

"No work is more important than the love of humankind."

"The great inspiration is that the work is oriented to the future. . . . Our job is to help young people build and prepare themselves for the future."

"I want to make a better world, a better city. We underestimate our potential to do things that leave a legacy."

Changemakers get their start in a number of different ways. I think it's one of the best pieces of news from the research. Just like there is no one ideal personality type to be a successful changemaker, there is no one best way to start on this path. We might be inspired by someone, we might get nominated by someone. We might feel we have nothing to lose. We might feel that we're hard-wired for this work. How you got here doesn't matter. What matters is that you ARE here, and you want to make a difference.

Your turn:

What is the story about where you got your changemaking start? Or, if you're brand-new to this, what is nudging you to get started?

What seed got planted early on? Who planted it?

What needs or gaps exist that could use a solution?

End of Section Reflection

What are your top two take-aways from this section on How Changemakers Perceive Themselves?

Section 2

HOW CHANGEMAKERS
RELATE TO OTHERS

I'm not a natural collaborator. When I develop something new, my default is to go it alone. One, I don't like to impose on others for help. Two, it seems like a lot of work to ask for input, arrange discussions, and synthesize all the feedback. Three, I've had a long-held belief that it's weak to ask for assistance; I'm competent and capable and can do it on my own.

When the research showed that successful changemakers actively seek to collaborate, I fought the impulse to make sense of the data myself, and I sought help. I shifted from a deficiency mindset (I can't do it on my own and I need help) to an elevation mindset (the result will be better if I work with others, and I *want* help).

How changemakers relate to, engage with, and view others, is key to their success. Whether the others are positive, helpful influences, or negative, detracting voices, changemakers navigate relationships with others in ways that foster win-win scenarios for all parties.

ASK FOR HELP AND COLLABORATE

One of the most powerful themes from the research is that people do not do this work—becoming changemakers or building changemakers—successfully on their own. The changemakers had several examples about what they've gotten help with, who they go to for help, and the approaches for collaboration that they think work best. But the bottom line is that they advise not to go it alone.

Changemakers offered their rationale for working with others:

- **Better productivity**—the amount of changemaking/philanthropic or paid work that can be achieved multiplies when we work with others.
- **Increased satisfaction**—talking about ideas with others is energizing.
- **Protects against naysayers**—involving others and building a community helps to create ownership among a group of stakeholders who are also invested in the outcome.
- **Helps with accountability**—other people will force you forward. If you are alone, you can give up.

"If you feel you're alone in your journey, it's easier to turn around and head back. I'm also a runner. It's easy to talk myself out of the run, but when there's someone else there, it keeps you in it."

The changemakers have ample advice for how best to involve others in their projects and initiatives:

Work with like-minded people: This does not mean to gather a group of 'yes-people' who agree with everything you say and don't challenge you; quite the opposite. What changemakers most value is having people around them who they respect, who they are inspired by, and who remind them of their principles. Changemakers look for people who share similar values and belief systems, who are also excited about the work, and who share common goals and a team-based approach. Changemakers also lean toward people who are positive and think of possibilities, versus people who spend time coming up with reasons why something won't work.

"You can only bring about change when you have a small army of people who help and who inspire."

Work with people who will hold you accountable: Who are the people you are willing to get feedback from? Who do you trust to challenge you? Who won't be shy about holding you accountable? In an article she wrote for *O, The Oprah Magazine*, Elizabeth Gilbert shared her four-question litmus test for how she chooses her trusted allies: "Do I trust this person's taste and judgment? Does this person understand what I'm trying to create here? Does this person genuinely want me to succeed? Is this person capable of delivering the truth to me in a sensitive and compassionate manner?" (Gilbert, 2017, para. 9).

What do you need to know about
the people you trust to hold you accountable?

Find people to fill the gaps: This is related to the theme of knowing your own strengths and weaknesses, because changemakers advise working with people who are skilled and talented, and who can do the things you cannot. Some people feel threatened when surrounded by others who are smart and talented, but for changemakers, the success of the cause is the ultimate goal, so working with the very best people makes sense in support of that end. Some of the attributes to look for include: expertise, specific skillsets, dedication, enthusiasm, and if they are a good match for you and for others you're working with.

"Take the time to find people with both the skills and the enthusiasm."

"Hire for attitude, train for knowledge."

Be respectful of those you're working with: Changemakers have learned over time that their trusted allies are their most important resource and should be treated that way. This includes involving others, even in start-up or program design conversations, allowing them to express their ideas and feelings in a safe environment, listening to a variety of different perspectives, showing appreciation, and sharing results. Changemakers admit that it's not always easy to be inclusive in conversations and show patience waiting for others to catch up to your leaps in thinking, but they report that it is worth it.

Another aspect of the collaborative mindset is to view potential collaborators as potential partners, and not as competitors. For example, it can be beneficial to look at how others' work may complement your own work, versus thinking of them as intruding on your space in the sector or field. In fact, some changemakers are advocates of not reinventing the wheel, but rather of looking at what others are doing, seeing what works, and adapting it to their situation. What else is out there that is close to your idea? What is someone else doing that is already working?

"It is amazing what you can accomplish if you do not care who gets the credit." Harry S. Truman

Your turn:

Where are you on the lone wolf–collaborator continuum?

What would a shift toward the collaborator side look like?

What collaboration opportunities exist for you right now?

What could you achieve through simply having coffee with others?

Who do you trust to challenge you?

MAINTAIN RELATIONSHIPS

Closely tied to the theme of asking for help and collaborating is a more general piece of advice about maintaining relationships. Changemakers are quite clear that how they view others is all about building and sustaining good relationships. Whether they speak about collaborators, employees, clients, or other stakeholders, changemakers hold relationships as critically important. Treating people well, offering kindness and compassion, respecting others' opinions, and being sensitive to the needs of others, are all elements of healthy relationships.

I specifically asked the interviewees where they turn when they need help, and while some folks mentioned books and other resources, almost all changemakers did not hesitate in reporting asking for help from spouses, other family members, friends, and colleagues. Many changemakers mentioned that seeking help from people they feel they can trust is key. Many admitted that holding a CEO, Executive Director, or other leadership position, can feel lonely. Having trusted advisors and confidantes—even those who are not necessarily subject-matter experts, but who can see situations objectively and offer new perspectives in thinking about situations—are incredibly valuable. Even competitors—when there is trust present in the relationship—can be helpful advisors. Other sources of help include coaches, mentors, experts, consultants, teachers, support groups, and professional conferences.

Your turn:

Where do you turn when you need help?

How easy is it for you to ask?

What might be stopping you from asking for help?

What needs to be in place for you to ask for help or support?

When asking for help, how do you know what to ask for?

FIND A MENTOR

One of the pieces of advice that arose several times in the interviews was to find a mentor, and later to be a mentor. Changemakers' tips for finding a mentor include: choosing someone you trust and admire; choosing someone who inspires you to make a difference; working with a senior or more experienced changemaker.

The more seasoned changemakers I interviewed spoke about the importance of becoming a mentor. Their perspective is that mentors are important for everyone, and that eventually they shifted from being inspired to inspiring others. They take great joy in being mentors for aspiring changemakers, waking up each day and being excited about helping others make a positive impact. Many spoke about how age doesn't matter for being a changemaker, but rather how energizing it is to work with younger people due to their idealism and energy to make change.

"It's just fabulous work, and it's the opportunity to work with young people. As you get older, people become gentler and magnanimous, but people also become cynical and mean-spirited. When you work with young people, there's not much room for cynicism; they're idealistic. I happen to be a great fan of the coming generations. I don't share some people's pessimism."

NAVIGATING NAYSAYERS

How do changemakers handle naysayers?

Naysayers are the real-life people who give destructive feedback, and who serve as obstacles on the road to making positive change. (This is different than our own negative inner dialogue and our own limiting beliefs, which are also obstacles and could be described as a different sort of naysayer. But the people who stand in our way are the naysayers referenced here.)

Naysayers can be the holders of red tape, as well as the gatekeepers of rules and societal conventions. They sometimes show up in the form of bosses, clients, and family. They can reveal themselves through the expectations they have, the lack of trust they experience (often fear-based), and the beliefs they cling to.

Changemakers, however, are not deterred. They have a healthy and mature outlook on naysayers, and they intentionally choose to make the naysayers' feedback work for them. This advanced perspective on naysayers is not my default, but I am learning (although I have a long way to go). Thank goodness the changemakers admitted that their responses to naysayers have evolved over time, too. Many reported that how they now handle naysayers is different than it used to be. For example, some changemakers report that in the past they would have been inclined to try to convince the doubters—to change the naysayers' minds. Now, in the present, those changemakers say that they don't attempt to change the minds of naysayers anymore, but rather they listen and utilize the feedback that is helpful.

"I don't spend a lot of time hitting my head against a stone wall."

How changemakers navigate the negativity involves a few elements:

In keeping with their general mindset to never stop learning, **changemakers regard naysayers' comments with a sincere curiosity, and they integrate what is useful**. They consider the feedback and evaluate if it is valid and valuable. They do not dismiss negative feedback outright, but rather discern if it could be helpful in sparking new or better ideas, complementing their existing work, or building a stronger case for the change.

Changemakers are motivated by the naysayers. In his Bigger Game model, Rick Tamlyn (2013) identifies allies as *sometimes* the people who cheer us on and are our best supporters, and *sometimes* the people whose negativity serves as fuel for our motivation fire. Changemakers agree: naysayers can help to strengthen their convictions, can serve as a launching pad or a motivator, can help to remind them of how much resilience they have, or can even provide an opportunity to build resilience skills.

"If you don't have naysayers, your mission isn't strong enough."

Being motivated to continue making a difference helps changemakers to stay focused on their cause, and they know that the results themselves will be what attracts the naysayers and brings them around in the end.

Changemakers sometimes collaborate with naysayers. This is a tricky one because the trap is to spend too much time and energy trying to join forces with folks who are committed to criticizing, instead of focusing on making the change. But changemakers recognize that sometimes you need to work with naysayers, especially if they will be a major obstacle. This could involve persevering and having discussions with naysayers, sharing information with them, and including them in decision-making. Some changemakers realize that, by collaborating, they increase their credibility and support, so setting aside their ego is worth it to accomplish the change goals.

Naysayers can serve as reminders to spend time finding supporters. Many changemakers opt to focus on people who share their optimism and who see the same opportunities. Even in the face of naysayer voices, they realize there are enough people who *are* aligned and who *do* support the work; they understand they don't need a majority to get started; and they remember that there are silent voices who are rallying them on.

Changemakers respect naysayers and understand this is simply how they view the world. This is one of the research findings that surprised me the most. Instead of taking the negativity personally, or letting the negativity take the wind out of their sails, changemakers genuinely respect the people who offer the feedback and simply view it as a different perspective. The best quote for this outlook comes from interviewee Joyce Odidison, a coach in Winnipeg, Manitoba, Canada. Her words truly capture this nuanced, advanced approach for perceiving naysayers and their negativity:

> I've learned to accept that's their job. It's not about me. It's their job and that's what they need to do to feel they're contributing. They don't always mean bad, their intentions aren't always necessarily evil or to put us down or scare us; that's the lens through which they see the world. They are trying to be helpful or prevent us from failure. . . . We all see the world differently, and we're all wired differently. If they're wired to be afraid of taking risks, they don't have to be aligned, but I need to go back and see if I am aligned or if that is right for me.
>
> What is right for me? Is [their perspective] my path? Does [their reaction] feel right? If not, thank them for what they've shared. . . . Your role in my life—that's your way of sharing knowledge, I appreciate it, but at this time, it's not a good fit for me. It's not really negative; that's their vision and their capacity—it's up to you to decide if it's a good fit or not. How many gifts have you had where it's a nice thought but you can't really use it? I think that's what naysayers are in our life. They come to test us, so we can really find out who we are . . . It confirms who I am on the path I need to walk. I may be the only one on the path, but that's okay for now.

When I asked about specific pieces of advice that interviewees would offer aspiring changemakers, I heard a number of statements about how to handle naysayers:

- Don't quit and be discouraged; find a different way.
- Think of it as water off a duck's back.
- Take opinions from a range of people, then let your heart decide.
- Spend your energy on what you *can* control.
- Keep a positive outlook and you won't be limited by obstacles.
- Don't take it personally.
- Believe in what you're doing.

"If I had listened to naysayers, I would've only done a quarter of everything I've accomplished."

Your turn:

What is your current belief about naysayers?

What do you notice about how you respond to their feedback?

What's the gift of the naysayer?

"Imagine you're at an antique flea market. Everything there has value—to someone—but not everything there has value to you. So you can recognize that it all has value, and your job is to figure out which items are valuable to you." (M. Casey, personal communication, July 11, 2017)

What would be YOUR metaphor for how you discern value from a wide variety of positive and negative feedback and input? (Your own example, like the flea market one.)

AUTHENTIC COMMUNICATION

One practical theme that arose from the interviews is the importance of communication. Changemakers know that it's not a good thing to be the best kept secret. It's important to communicate well at all times and through a variety of media.

Telling the story of success is one element of this theme. Whether it be through social media, your website, or other channels, sharing the news and information about your project is key. For one thing, the act of articulating your story helps you to get clarity on your vision and the service you provide. Beyond the content or 'What' of your message, however, is 'How' you deliver it. For example, how you communicate tough messages will tell people about your character, and will hopefully give people reason to trust you and your organization.

One of my first teaching experiences was in the College of Engineering at the University of Saskatchewan. I was on a team of instructors who all taught the same course: Oral and Written Communication for Engineering Students. It wasn't an easy sell for that audience, although some students would later admit—after some work experience—that while their job involved using their engineering skills, they also needed the skills to *communicate* the engineering to non-engineers.

Our team of instructors was led by a brilliant woman, Jennifer MacLennan. Dr. MacLennan is a specialist in rhetoric, and she taught our team of instructors to teach the communication course from the perspective of rhetoric, based on the foundation set out by Aristotle. Now, I don't remember much from those workshops that Dr. MacLennan facilitated for us, but I do remember the handy triangle model she provided:

She said that Aristotle asserted that there are three ways a speaker can influence an audience: logos (logically sound arguments), ethos (the character the speaker displays), and pathos (what the listener or receiver of the message values, hopes for, needs, and fears).

Dr. MacLennan told us that another way of looking at the points of the triangle is: message, speaker, and receiver. For many people the lion's share of their time is spent on crafting the *message*—ensuring we're using the perfect words to build the best logical communication. She said that sometimes we expend some effort to consider our role as the *speaker*—*how* we want to approach communicating our message. (J. MacLennan, personal communication, January, 2001)

But, in my experience, what is lacking most is our attention on the *receiver* of our message. What is important to them? What do they want from the communication? What are they hoping for?

The changemakers may not have articulated the elements using the terms logos, ethos, and pathos, but they did talk about the importance of clear, consistent messaging, warmth and sincerity when they communicate it, and communicating in a way that will speak to the audience.

Being authentic in your communication is essential for building trust. Changemakers encourage communicating with passion, as it helps to engage others with their cause, but the passion needs to be genuine for you. Some changemakers believe that the most important thing you sell is *you*. So, being consistent with messaging and with your personal approach is essential. And no matter how much we depend on technology, changemakers argue that connecting with others in-person or via technologies where we can see and hear one another is still important. Humans are wired for connection, after all, so being visible and engaged with stakeholders is a wise investment.

While the idea of communication may so far seem easy, one tangential aspect that some changemakers approach with trepidation is cultivating a public profile. When I asked changemakers what would make their work more satisfying, they responded, almost universally, that having a wider impact on more people would make it better. And while changemakers are not tied to being at the center of it all, they do know that instigators of change get put in the public eye. The public can be interested in a change-maker's origins, what she is passionate about, where she has struggled, and what she takes a stand for.

When I gave an early version of this manuscript to beta readers, they all told me—independent of one another—that they wanted more of *me* in the book. I resisted this feedback for a long time (the results of the research are compelling on their own; this isn't about me; I'm not that interesting anyway; etc.). But they wanted to know more about my story, how I relate to the research themes, and what my experience has been through the project.

One lesson I'm learning is that part of authentic communication is communicating openly and honestly about one's own experience. And when one puts her personal story out there, building resilience for this phenomenon is in order. I find it beneficial to follow the lead of those I interviewed: changemakers simply remember that the change is not about them, it's about making a difference for others, so putting the focus on the cause itself seems to help. (Refer to Feeling Fear and Taking Action Anyway in Section Three for more on this.)

Your turn:

How do you tell the story of the change you are making?

How do you recognize what your audience wants or needs to hear?

What else might your audience want to know that you haven't addressed yet?

What are your best strategies for communicating authentically?

End of Section Reflection

What is one thing you want to remember from this section on How Changemakers Relate to Others?

Section 3
HOW CHANGEMAKERS
ORIENT THEMSELVES TO ACTION

"If you have a dream, you can spend a lifetime studying, planning, and getting ready for it. What you should be doing is getting started." Drew Houston

Those who are successfully changing the world—or their piece of the world—are oriented to take action. Otherwise they wouldn't be successful. Lots of us work hard on getting better clarity on our vision and purpose, and we do look to others for help, but it's the getting out there and taking action that can be the show-stopper.

The thought of writing this book was a show-stopper for me for quite some time. It was only with the smallest of steps that I was able to move forward. One of my all-time favourite quotes comes from Thomas Carlyle: "Go as far as you can see; when you get there, you'll be able to see further." Early on, I could only see as far as simply setting a word count goal for each day and just sitting still and typing. After the first draft was finished, "as far as I could see" was speaking with local authors to find out how they turned their Word document into a book they could hold in their hands. And on it went, step by step.

Looking back over the last two years, I notice this pattern repeating: I don't know how to do it, I learn about it, and then I take a small step toward it. That's it. So this giant, how-will-I-ever-climb-this-Mount-Everest-of-a-project book finally happened. But only by the smallest of steps. I am literally going as far as I can see, and when I get *there*, I actually *can* see how to go further.

Changemakers know this. One of the most reassuring themes from the research is that successful changemakers don't have the whole thing figured out before they start. They take a small step, see how it goes, make any adjustments, and then step again. They are committed to their cause (or program or project or initiative) and they keep taking small actions.

START SOMEWHERE

One of my favourite questions in the changemaker interviews went something like this: "Lots of people have great ideas for how they want to make a difference or change the world. How did you go from having a great idea to actually taking action on it?"

The most popular answer was that they just got started.

"I took a small step."

"I needed to start somewhere."

"It started with one small, monumental step."

"Just do it; plans go astray because of a lack of implementation."

"I took control of me, because that's the only thing in my control."

"Less talk; take action."

"Take good ideas and do it."

You get the picture.

In terms of how to take this first step, the advice was plentiful. Changemakers recognize that starting is the hardest, but that it makes a difference to start small. The bottom line is at least to start somewhere.

Changemakers recognize that it can be the unknown that scares people from starting, so they advocate giving ourselves permission to go into it without knowing everything. They remind us to remember that we are part of something bigger, and to push past the fear. They are honest about making it up as they go, so it doesn't have to be fully mapped out in order to begin creating. My friend and changemaker, Lori Maloney, shared this quote with me: "Imperfect action will always beat perfect inaction."

"When you pray, move your feet. When you have an idea, you have to do something about it. You've got to do something about it."

"Just do it. The best plans go astray because of lack of implementation. We see it all the time, everywhere. It's the implementation stage that fails—whether in personal life or in a corporate setting."

"Don't wait until your idea is fully formed and perfect. Don't wait until you've got a lot of people backing you and saying yes. Don't wait for other people to tell you it's a great idea."

"The turning point for me was 'let's just make it up.' The more I started to meet people in esteemed leadership positions, the more I realized they're just making it up, and I can make it

up as I go along, too. I started to make outlines and timelines and stopped buying into needing to have it handled before I step into it. I started to create it first . . . We don't have it all handled and we can still be extraordinary."

Your turn:

What's stopping you from getting started or taking the next step?

What permission do you need to give yourself to get started or take the next step?

What one small action would have the greatest impact on the positive difference you wish to make?

OVERCOMING OBSTACLES

In addition to reporting themselves and their own limiting beliefs as their biggest obstacle, changemakers spoke about a wide variety of external obstacles they have encountered, including:

- lack of funds;
- limiting mindsets held by others;
- bureaucracy, political situation, regulations;
- societal conventions and old rules;
- having lots of ideas and choosing what to do next;
- staff turnover; and
- life commitments (family, home).

The interviews didn't reveal a crisp solution to each of the obstacles, but rather provided a few approaches for how to think about the obstacles and overcome them.

Lack of funding was a common obstacle for many changemakers and, for the most part, they reported that this circumstance was a motivator of sorts. In other words, because of their deep commitment to their cause, changemakers found that the lack of resources spurred them to work harder. Their solutions to the lack of funding included:

- diversify the sources of funding and get everyone involved in the effort;
- increase creativity to develop new solutions in times of adversity; and

- streamline and narrow the focus during a downturn to remain profitable or viable.

"If we would've had an angel investor up front, the quality of our program would be lower. By struggling and communicating our impact and results over extended periods of time, we were forced to refine our program down to its highest quality potential."

This quote illustrates one of the changemakers' best abilities: they turn obstacles into opportunities. They spoke about going around, under, or over obstacles, and also about going after them, with tenacity and vigour. They reported being persistent and staying calm, setting boundaries, and getting clear on where to compromise and where not to. Finally, they advocated simply doing the best they could, and not letting setbacks stop them.

"Just set your goals and take feedback from the environment. Don't throw your hands up; be aware there is going to be a delay in the world for the change you're working for. Have patience. Bruce Lee said, be water. Water doesn't stop at a rock or an obstacle, it finds other ways. Be effortless and look for the other path."

"We haven't the money, so we've got to think."
Ernest Rutherford

"There is good in everything, if only we look for it." Laura Ingalls Wilder

Your turn:

What external obstacles are currently in your way?

When do you let obstacles stop you?

What are your best strategies for overcoming barriers?

FEELING FEAR AND TAKING ACTION ANYWAY

Early on in the research it was apparent that changemakers approach risks and perceive courage in a unique way. They have doubts and are scared like the rest of us, but they find a way to get past it. In other words, changemakers certainly feel fear, but they take action anyway.

The work is not what anyone else is doing. Changemakers are quite clear that they are heading down a different path than most people, taking a new direction, and thinking differently. Changemakers realize that not only are they not *doing* what anyone else is doing, they themselves are *not like* what anyone else is like. Being alone on a path can lead to feeling fear, but changemakers find a way to forge ahead anyway.

"Realize you're your own human being and you're here for a reason and here to make a ripple. If you go along with everyone else, you nullify your contribution/existence/impact. Chart your own path and your own course. Go for it, do what feels right."

It helps to remember your purpose. This can be a vulnerable place, charting new territory. Where many of us may read the poster about being brave, and then keep hesitating, changemakers show up with bravery. They remember why they are doing it. They do it because it makes sense and because it's the right thing to do. (Refer to Remember Your Bigger Why later in this section to learn more.)

Changemakers are not afraid to fail. Part of this comes from their discipline of not spending time thinking about the downside. Unlike many of us, they are not immobilized by fear or by rejection. They simply believe that it is better to try and fail than not try at all. In keeping with their predisposition to learning, they view failures as learning experiences where they gain more information about how to take the next steps.

Step out of the expectations others have of you. Expectations placed on us by others can be heavy and difficult to shed. Changemakers recognize that they were under such constraints and that they needed to step out of them. They re-invented themselves, they created a job title when there was no existing category, and they created something new when there was no pre-existing model. For some changemakers, this can be exciting: a time when new creativity within is awoken, and when they feel they are more aligned with who they are, and not with someone else's version of who they are or who they should be.

Step out of your comfort zone. Changemakers are quite aware they have a comfort zone and that they have needed to step out of it in order to lead the change. Sometimes they refer to this as "stepping outside my element," taking risks, taking chances, being uncomfortable. What helps is having a toolbox of tactics to help overcome what's difficult.

"An obstacle that is still real for me is networking in large groups where I don't know anybody. I am not good at small

talk and least of all large group chit chat. I have nothing to say and can't relate to the conversation. . . . I much prefer a one-on-one and to have a real conversation. Yet I go to networking events and try hard to connect, however uncomfortable. I go with someone else so that I'm not alone, so I have a home base to go back to. Hopefully there's a few people I know who can introduce me. Instead of me feeling like I have to make it happen, I stand back and see who comes to me— sometimes they do, and sometimes they don't. It's nice when they do."

A few years ago, I enrolled in the positive psychology coaching certification course through Robert Biswas-Diener and his Positive Acorn company. I loved that program. We were challenged to look beyond the surface of classic positive psychology messages and pursue a deeper understanding of the nuances of the research, as well as practice applying positive psychology techniques in live coaching demonstrations. One of the course topics was courage. Robert referred to his book, *The Courage Quotient: How Science Can Make You Braver* (Biswas-Diener, 2012). He defines courage as someone choosing to act when they experience the conditions of being afraid, the outcome is uncertain, and there is a personal threat present. He told us that the personal risk doesn't necessarily have to be a physical threat, and that the fear of social rejection is just as powerful as the fear of falling off a cliff. The courage quotient itself is one's willingness to act divided by one's fear, and that the willingness to act only needs to be a bit larger than the fear. So, the trick then is knowing that we can adjust either of these factors, either increasing willingness to act, or decreasing fear.

To help reduce the fear of social rejection, Robert told us that what helps is to shift from an internal focus to an external focus where we remember how we are in service, and why it is important in the world. (R. Biswas-Diener, personal communication, October 29, 2013)

Changemakers know this. They remember that their passion, their purpose, and what compels them, are the life rafts that keep them afloat when the water gets choppy. They focus less on themselves and more on the project, clients, or outcomes. To help reduce the fear of failure, Robert told us that it can help to focus on incremental progress, celebrating small wins, and being intentional about pausing to reflect on where we were and on how far we've come.

To help increase one's willingness to act, we can create "low stakes failure." One example is to take small steps instead of giant leaps, or to practice a presentation in front of trusted allies (or in front of a mirror) before delivering it to the real audience. Changemakers know this, too. They talked about helping one person at a time, standing on the sidelines and first observing, and starting with baby steps.

Changemakers are not invincible beings who only experience confidence and bravery and never feel fear or doubt. They are humans who have found a way to get over the discomfort and press on for the sake of the change they are trying to make.

"We generate from: 1) the pain is so great I must change it, or 2) I am so compelled by this I want to share it. For millions of us, we get caught in the middle: it's good enough, don't change, don't rock the boat. I'm not willing to lose what I have—the comfort zone. 'I-could-lose-what-I-have averse.' People are loss averse, not risk averse.... The unintended impact of success is: the more successful we become, the less risk we want to take. We're attached to what we have. So it's the founding energy of, 'I've got nothing to lose, there's nothing in the bank.'"

Your turn:

What are you doing (or believe you need to do) that nobody else is doing?

When do you feel fear? What situation is currently causing you to feel fear?

What's the risk of taking action?

Try this way to assess risk: What's the worst-case scenario? How likely is it to happen? How bad would that be, really?

What's your motivation for taking the risk? Who are you serving?

What will encourage you to 'set yourself aside' in order to serve this higher purpose?

HAVE PATIENCE

Changemakers are almost unanimous in their assertion that having patience is essential. For some it's about being resilient and persevering over time; for others it's about being patient with folks who may need to catch up. For almost all it's about knowing that change doesn't always happen quickly—and we need to be okay with that. For many changemakers this isn't easy because they are results-oriented, but they also know that sometimes there are 'delays in the feedback loop.' There aren't always clear impacts seen in the short term, because ideas take time to catch on and become adopted, and because the conditions of readiness need to be there.

Some of the best advice is simply to be patient and persevere.

"If you want to make change, it's not going to happen on your time line. The world doesn't belong to you. It belongs to the universe, and the universe will decide when it's going to happen. You can help it along but it's not going to happen on your time line. Don't give up."

"You have to have contained impatience. You need to have impatience, but you cannot manifest that at every turn."

BE DETERMINED AND PERSEVERE

Closely tied to the theme of patience is the advice to be determined and persevere. Patience refers to the element of time, and of things taking longer than we might want or expect. Determination and perseverance refer to sticking with it even when it gets hard (stick-to-it-iveness).

Changemakers do not sugar coat situations; they are not shy about admitting how challenging the work can be. Words used to describe the level of difficulty and discomfort are: "exhausting"; "I didn't know what I was doing"; "I started with nothing"; "it seemed insurmountable." With an equal amount of conviction, changemakers also emphasized the importance of determination:

- Be relentless.
- Be persistent.
- Keep plugging along.
- Keep persevering.
- Consider where it's best to direct your energy.
- Stick with it.
- Sometimes it's sheer will.
- Never give up.
- Commit fully.
- Have commitment over the long term.
- It takes a high level of sustained effort.
- Be willing to roll up your sleeves and work hard.
- Be brave when it's hardest.

"Choose something and keep sculpting it over your life. Keep sculpting your own one project because that is how you become a master. I closed my eyes and imagined my son. My son is 10 and he makes movies and if he ever stops, it would be heartbreaking. What he needs to do, he needs to keep making movies, and the biggest heartbreak would be if someone told him it wasn't any good and he stopped. It's what happens to us: someone tells us it sucks and so we stop."

HAVE FAITH

In general, changemakers spoke about faith as a type of trust. The faith that changemakers reported isn't necessarily religious faith (although some spoke about turning to their religious faith in difficult times and using daily prayer to stay focused). It seems that keeping the faith is another life preserver to keep us afloat when we might otherwise drown in worry. "Have faith that things will work out." "Have faith in what you are doing." "Have faith that the solutions or answers will come to you." "Apply faith when taking a risk." "Trust in the power of the universe. The universe only has good in store for you."

Your turn:

What helps to build your patience?

What helps you persevere 'when the going gets tough'?

What are the types of faith you rely on?

BE OPEN TO CHANGES AND TO DIFFERENT RESULTS

Here's some irony: changemakers know that they themselves need to be open to things turning out differently than they expected. In other words, they need to stay open to change. Many changemakers refer to this as being open to unexpected opportunities that present themselves. Similar to their perspective that there aren't really failures, only more chances to keep learning, changemakers know that unforeseen outcomes are new openings for making a difference.

"Have a fluid identity, don't be stuck on how it should look, be open to having your desires delivered in unfamiliar forms."

In 2009, Ben Dooley, a brilliant master-level coach from Chicago, wrote an unforgettable article about the difference between commitment and attachment, and he relayed his experience of writing a book.

> What we're talking about in part is the difference between 'Commitment' and 'Attachment.'
>
> Don't get me wrong, I'm not saying 'Attachment' is bad. By all means, if it works for you, then go for it. But most of the time when we form attachments to a specific outcome, we end up feeling frustrated, limited, and penned in. It's where that dreaded 'fear of failure' begins to arise and take command.
>
> And it's also how we end up getting derailed and therefore we end up having a really difficult

time accomplishing our goals, and almost always we just end up letting them drop away. Look at my experience with the book. If I had really locked in and was determined to have my book out by July 2008 as I had originally intended, I'm sure I could have done it. But that would have been fulfilling the attached outcome of 'having a simple five- to 10-page eBook' . . .

But as it turns out, that wasn't the compelling goal. For me this time, the real goal was to 'create and provide a book that shared essential knowledge and experience to other coaches, helping them in the beginning stages of building their coaching business.' That being the case, I have something more compelling to focus on and help guide me, especially those times when I'm getting stuck . . .

What made this journey a whole lot easier was to let go of some of the goals (completed by a certain time), while connecting with stronger more compelling goals (provide learning and value). In other words, letting go of the 'attachment' of how it was 'supposed to be' and focusing on my 'commitment.' (Dooley, 2009, para. 9-11)

Recently, Ben generously shared with me some of his additional, deeper insights on this valuable distinction:

If we look through the lens of everything we do—all our actions and reactions are based on and inspired by either Fear or Love—then we can also apply this to the world of Commitment VS. Attachment.

When we are Attached to a Result, there are invariably a few fears that are involved—what happens if it doesn't work out the way I want? What if something else happens? And what horrible bad things will happen if I don't get what I want? We have set our sights on a very narrow outcome that is also tied in to consequences.

The other thing to consider is that when we are triggered by some sort of threat or danger—thus activating our fears—we also revert to a form of 'Fight, Flight or Freeze,' which means that we literally lose the ability to think creatively and intelligently and explore possibility.

As a result, we have placed ourselves into an unwinnable trap. We've added additional pressure upon ourselves, thus increasing the threat, thus making it harder to think and act powerfully, thus making it harder to actually achieve the very thing that we are working so hard to achieve.

Now looking at the world of Commitment. In this case, our intentional, purposeful, meaningful, fulfilling commitments—the ones we *choose* to make. What we are really experiencing is a deep connection to our Values—experiencing and expressing ourselves in the pursuit of a particular outcome and experience.

Well, when we are fully engaged with our Values, we are open to other possibilities and outcomes.

This is where exciting and amazing things are created and discovered—often beyond our original and limited way of thinking. We are open to new ideas and collaboration.

Being Committed to an outcome provides us with the support and structure to recover from failure. If we are attached to a specific and narrow result, then we are putting ourselves in a WIN/ LOSE situation—either you did it or you didn't. And if you did it, congratulations. And if you didn't, then you FAIL!

When we are Committed to an Outcome and Experience, then when we meet obstacles, when we fall down, when we get stopped and when we fail, we are much more easily able to pick ourselves up, discover what was missing, and get ourselves back on track. (B. Dooley, personal communication, July 10, 2019)

Changemakers understand this, too. They can be committed to their purpose or vision or what compels them, but they don't need to stay attached to how it will turn out. In fact, when we are unattached to specific outcomes, more possibilities may become apparent, because we're open-minded, not closed to new ideas.

"We're romanced into the notion that everything is significant and true, and it isn't always. Don't pretend that you need to know the answers. When I am so attached to getting the answer right, it messes everything up."

In other words, changemakers are open to thinking of their work as an experiment. They are open to giving something a try and then learning from the outcome—because the learning informs their next go.

"Some people would want to have the plan perfect—but we were very fluid—we had a notion of what progress looked like, and if it felt like progress, we went with it. Over the years we've had to cull some things, things that didn't work. It was a mistake, you move on. Dispassionately. You start the effort and, if you see it's not going to work, drop it and move on."

"I am willing to critically evaluate what I'm doing and recognize when I need to change gears, switch, or dismantle and start over."

For changemakers, being open also means having the humility to know that their way is not the only way. Being open-minded to others' suggestions, approaches, and ways of doing things is important, as is being open to ideas coming from a variety of sources. According to changemakers, ideas can come from quotes, poems, songs, nature, and simply allowing time to pass while looking for new perspectives.

Your turn:

What is the big-picture goal you are committed to?

What are you currently attached to?

How might some attachments be serving you?

Where are your attachments holding you back?

How do you remain open to fluid conditions and results?

NO REGRETS, BUT START EARLIER

The very first time I presented the results of this research, someone asked me, "What *didn't* you see in the results that surprised you?" That question stopped me in my tracks. I answered that, on recall, I didn't see or hear any regrets.

During the interviews, I specifically asked, "What would you do differently?"

Changemakers were quite clear in their responses that everything—mistakes and mis-steps included—had led them to this point and, therefore, there were no regrets.

This isn't to say their experience over time was error-free and perfect. Not at all: changemakers are upfront about admitting their blunders. But, upon looking back, they choose to focus on the overall journey and what they learned, instead of dwelling on what went wrong. This perspective includes:

- Yes, there are mistakes and obstacles, but you learn from them and move forward.
- These experiences help with focus; you can build on it; it's all part of the journey.
- Take the good from the situation and grow from it; it can alter your path and feed the goal.
- It has made me what I am today.
- I wouldn't change the experiences I've had.
- Look at it as an opportunity, re-evaluate, and step forward again.
- It can be hard to see it at the time.

The only comment that could be construed as 'regret' was changemakers' nearly unanimous sentiment that they should have started earlier. In general, hindsight provided the ability to recognize that what stopped them in the early days was some sort of fear, and they wish they would've gotten over that fear sooner.

The fear, of course, takes on different forms, and some of the examples of what they wish they could've done earlier include:

- I wish I was an earlier bloomer; I would've started sooner.
- I could've started giving back earlier.
- I would've spent more time writing and less time on the day job.
- I would've admitted sooner that I don't know it all.
- I would've taken a creator stance versus victim stance earlier.
- I would've gotten help sooner (hire consultants, seek a mentor).
- I would've done the scary stuff faster.
- I would've gotten alignment between my work and my values earlier.
- I would've left an abusive boss earlier.
- I would've trusted myself more.

The calling, the urge to do this work, the unrelenting voice in our head . . . there is no question that the pull is there. It's undeniable. And what stops us is almost always a form of fear. So is trust the antidote?

Your turn:

What would be different if you trusted yourself?

If you trusted yourself to take a first step, what would that look like?

What are you putting off starting?

REMEMBER YOUR BIGGER WHY

Martin Parnell is an ordinary guy who does extraordinary things. He resides in Alberta, Canada, and is a prime example of a changemaker. In 2010, Mr. Parnell ran 250 marathons in that one calendar year. That is a stunning feat.

In September of 2010, Mr. Parnell spoke to our Calgary Chapter of the International Coaching Federation about his endeavour. He was funny, inspiring, and honest. He told us that his original goal was to run a marathon a day for a year, but that his medical team "talked him down" and encouraged him to build in some buffer days, which he did. So, with a goal of 250 marathons in one year, he explained how Monday to Friday were typically his running days, that Saturday was an eating day, and Sunday was a rest day (or something like that).

Someone in the audience asked him, "Mr. Parnell, you have been following this gruelling schedule for over eight months now. How in the world do you swing your legs out of bed to run the next marathon every morning for five days each week?" Mr. Parnell did not hesitate to answer:

"Oh, I just remember why I'm doing it; I'm doing it for the kids." (M. Parnell, personal communication, September 15, 2010)

You see, in addition to the personal challenge of running these many marathons, Mr. Parnell had an ulterior motive: he was using his quest to raise money for a charity called Right To Play, whose mission is to "Protect, educate and empower children to rise above adversity using the power of play" (Right To Play, 2020, About Us section). His goal was to raise $250,000. The final total was $320,000.

Mr. Parnell did not stop there. He has pursued a number of other quests and challenges for the purpose of raising more funds and making a positive difference in the world. You can learn more at his website: www.martinparnell.com

One of the biggest lessons I learned from Martin Parnell is the power of remembering one's bigger Why. One of the questions I asked the changemakers was, "What motivates you to keep doing the work day after day, even when it gets crappy and hard?" The predominant answer was that changemakers remind themselves of the reasons they are doing this work. Whether they referred to it as their passion that keeps them going, or that they're doing it for the "right reasons," or that they have a higher purpose, changemakers believe in the power of remembering why this work is important. They report that staying connected to the broader purpose sustains them in difficult times. Here is their advice for how to connect with what's important:

- Stay true to—and be aligned with—your values.
- Take time and identify your purpose.
- Believe in what you do; have faith in what you are doing.
- Understand your drive. What's compelling? What are you passionate about? What fulfills you?

- Nurture and increase your desire for the work; it will decrease your fear.
- Do it for the right reasons: not for ego, but for others—not for external recognition, but because it makes sense.

They ask:

- What do you want to see in your world?
- What does your intuition or gut feeling tell you?
- What do you know "in your heart of hearts" is the right thing to do?
- Find a mission. If not you, then who else would do this work?

Goals: Changemakers are systematic in how they set their goals and work through their action plans. Spending time on the planning stage is recommended, including developing timelines. Setting benchmarks—and 'stretch goals'—and striving to meet them, is another valuable exercise, including reflecting at least annually on what was accomplished and where personal growth was seen.

Research: Some changemakers spoke about the importance of doing research. Having evidence-based information is valuable for building cases, developing business plans, creating programs, and making decisions. Sometimes, gathering evidence is also important in assessing risk and political will, in determining feasibility and practicality, and in revealing if the time is right. While setting goals is forward-looking, changemakers also gather information to get clarity on the current state, since that may inform goals and actions for how to equip themselves for success. Having evidence can also be crucial in convincing others and demonstrating a process that goes from the current reality to a new way of doing things.

Action: Changemakers did not talk about goal setting without also talking about taking action. They recognize that plans go astray because of a lack of implementation, and that sometimes what's needed is simply to push through and keep going when it gets hard (as that's usually when we stop). Staying laser focused on the right actions is also essential:

"You have to pause and take stock and check the environment and your activities. Be self-critical and take a look at what

you're doing and identify what and where you're doing well and not so well. I am self-critical, and I take stock of where I am frequently. I say this to the top managers: Are you sure you have the five most important files on your desk? Identify the right five files and stay on top of them all the time."

Some changemakers recognize that consistently taking baby steps is what makes the difference:

"I've always started with baby steps—very small steps. Whenever I have an idea, I start with just achievable little steps. That's how it was twenty years ago. I had a vision for a one-room school. I started with five students and it grew to 25, then it grew to 100. I start small . . . but I always assure myself that it has the potential to grow bigger. I actually vision it as a stairway. If the 25 are at the top of the stairs, when I have five I know I'm one-fifth of the way to achieving my goal—just four more steps."

Your turn:

What is your preferred goal-setting approach?

What helps you to get clarity on a vision?

What are the tactics or strategies that help you to stay on track through implementation?

CELEBRATE SUCCESSES

Some changemakers noted the importance of celebrating successes, including sharing successes with their teams. This isn't always easy. Sometimes, taking a break to recognize what's been accomplished, and celebrate it, flies in the face of speed, urgency, efficiency, and results. And yet pausing to acknowledge achievements and progress can serve as additional fuel and inspiration to keep the momentum going.

Changemakers shared different examples of what success looks like to them, spanning the wide variety of sectors and types of projects with which they are involved. Even so, several common themes emerged for what changemakers are proud of and what feels successful:

Client success: Overwhelmingly, changemakers report feeling most satisfied and successful when the people they serve are successful. This includes when those they're helping are happy, proud, or hopeful; when they succeed despite vulnerabilities; and when they grow, learn, and experience shifts in their thinking or behaviour.

Ripple effect: Many changemakers recognize that success comes in the form of a ripple effect: knowing that the people they help, in turn, go out and make a difference themselves. Examples include the youth they help who grow up and help others; individual clients who gain skills and self-esteem and become better parents, friends, and community members; and even team members who take on other roles to make a difference in the world.

The starfish story: Some changemakers referenced the starfish story:

> One day, an old man was walking along a beach that was littered with thousands of starfish that had been washed ashore by the high tide. As he walked he came upon a young boy who was eagerly throwing the starfish back into the ocean, one by one.
>
> Puzzled, the man looked at the boy and asked what he was doing. Without looking up from his task, the boy simply replied, "I'm saving these starfish, Sir."
>
> The old man chuckled aloud, "Son, there are thousands of starfish and only one of you. What difference can you make?"
>
> The boy picked up a starfish, gently tossed it into the water and turning to the man, said, "I made a difference to that one!" (Starfish Project, 2020, Our Story section)

Some changemakers are clear that success means helping one person at a time, not necessarily changing all of society. By focusing on individuals, changemakers can see how that investment pays off with a big impact. While scaling an operation to help the masses can have its benefits, there are also successes to be found in personalizing the service and offering a deeper level of help to fewer people.

Being recognized: While changemakers aren't motivated by external recognition, they do feel successful as they start developing a reputation for something meaningful. This includes being respected by peers and professional associations, and being recognized by wider award programs for giving to their communities and making a positive difference.

Seeing results: Some changemakers define success by the concrete results to which they contribute. For example, they feel proud of books they've published, reaching more and more people through a website, seeing positive financial results with fundraising, growing membership and effectiveness in professional associations, and observing when their own work is being used by others for doing good in the world.

Developing positive approaches: While changemakers take considerable pride in WHAT they achieve, they are also clearly proud of HOW they achieved it. In other words, the approach they use to achieve the results can be as important as the results themselves. Changemakers also reported feeling proud of the *evolution* of their approaches; they recognize their own development in becoming more effective with *how* they do their work over time and with experience. Examples include developing more patience and growing positive cultures within teams, client groups, and even within their own families.

Personal breakthroughs: Finally, changemakers pointed to how they achieved personal breakthroughs to illustrate a different type of success. They spoke about changing mindsets (both internal and external perceptions); having the courage to change tactics—both personal direction and long-standing organizational practices; finding their own voice; finding balance with all of life's responsibilities versus drowning in self-limiting beliefs; and discovering the freedom and fulfillment that comes with pursuing something they're passionate about.

"I've overcome obstacles by thinking differently about myself, redefining who I thought I was. The bravest thing I've ever done was becoming involved in wheelchair sport and deciding to become a parent. They both made me have to change the way I saw myself and identified myself. Long, historical, really deep-seated beliefs I had to change."

Your turn:

What about you? Out of everything you've done to make a difference in the world, what are you most proud of?

How do you define success?

And how do you celebrate it?

THE WORK IS NEVER DONE AND THE JOURNEY CONTINUES

I asked the changemakers, "What would make your work even more satisfying?" Their answers reflected their desire to give even more of themselves. They strive to do an even better job of making a positive difference for others and for their worlds. They are not ones to rest on their laurels; they can see that there is more to be done.

Have a greater impact: Overwhelmingly, what would make the work more satisfying for changemakers is if they could do even more, to have an even greater impact on more people. They want to raise more awareness of their cause, make more progress more quickly, and ensure the work will continue after they're gone.

"The tendency is that any path to change is a long one. I wish it was shorter."

Find more time: Changemakers also feel pressed for time. They would like to have more time for reflection, for working on all their ideas, for planning, and for tracking achievements, to name a few. They are quick to name solutions such as delegation or automation as potential ways to address the lack of time.

Find more resources: Many of the changemakers I spoke with work in the non-profit sector, and their work would be more satisfying if they weren't constantly worried about finances. They shared that more funds would allow them to help even more people. They have a desire to be mission driven—not capital driven—but they also recognize the need to be realistic. Changemakers are also self-aware, and acknowledge that a lack of predictability and consistency in funding is stressful, which is a difficult environment to thrive in.

Hear more feedback: As confident as changemakers are, they are still human, and receiving positive feedback that what they're doing is making a difference helps to keep them going. They admit that, in the absence of any feedback, it can be scary; not knowing how the work is being received can lead to self-doubt creeping in.

From wanting more time and additional resources, to finding ways to further champion, improve, and grow their bodies of work, changemakers are relentless in their pursuit to advance their cause or project. While they have been successful achieving certain milestones, changemakers' journeys never seem to be done.

End of Section Reflection

What is one take-away you want to remember from this section on How Changemakers Orient Themselves to Action?

CONCLUSION

WHO ARE THE CHANGEMAKERS?

The 48 people I interviewed come from different back-grounds and make a positive difference in a variety of ways. For some, their paid work is their changemaker work. Others work regular jobs and have volunteer changemaker roles. Still others do both paid changemaker work and volunteer changemaker work.

How they make a difference in the world is also varied.

Some are driven to change mindsets by helping individuals (for example: helping teens see themselves in new ways, or helping unemployed people to see opportunities instead of barriers), and some are hoping to change societal mindsets (for example: changing the perceptions which people have of and toward disability, or encouraging industry to see women as a solution to a labour shortage in the trades).

Some changemakers serve disadvantaged and under-privileged populations, and some help individuals build an increased capacity for effectiveness (for example:

reducing stress, increasing success for women entrepreneurs, increasing well-being for mothers, highlighting and capitalizing on the unique gifts and talents of employees and other team members).

Other changemakers lead change at a macro level, taking a community-wide perspective or a public policy focus.

By and large, changemakers are humble. The first question of every interview was: "Describe the difference you're making in the world/at work/in your community." The majority of changemakers prefaced their response with some version of, "I'm not sure I'm making a difference, but I hope that I am."

They are a confident group, to be sure, but they are not arrogant.

They view their changemaker identity in a variety of ways. Here are other responses to being asked to describe the difference they're making:

- The title of changemaker is tough to have.
- It's difficult to say you're making a difference because it's difficult to measure the difference.
- I have a humility gremlin; I have trouble with "I."
- That's very direct. Why didn't you ask, "What difference do you *hope* you're making?"
- Many days I don't think I am making a difference.
- I feel I am a gardener and I plant seeds patiently. I don't always know what difference I've made.
- I prefer the term "aspiring changemaker"; I like approaching it as a beginner.

- I was taught not to think of myself, but to think of others.
- This question is hard for people who are humble.
- I'd like to think I'm making a difference.

I also asked the changemakers: "I use this term 'changemaker' a lot. What term(s) do you use to describe yourself? How do others describe you?"

The total list of terms they provided spans two pages, but the most popular ones are:

- Visionary
- Leader
- Mentor
- Change agent
- Facilitator
- Activist
- Community builder
- Risk taker
- Innovator
- Catalyst
- Connector
- Pioneer
- Thought leader
- Changemaker

CLOSING REMARKS

The aim of this book is to encourage you to find the changemaker mindsets within yourself, and foster even more confidence in your abilities, so that you can boldly get out there and make a difference.

In the time since I started writing this book, I have been challenged to think about my project in new ways, while never losing sight of my mission to help you and many others be confident changemakers. While the book is complete, my own journey continues. What's next for me is to keep thinking of ways to make the research themes more relatable, to explore the relationship between the self-interest and collective interest of being a changemaker, and to find opportunities to share more of my own story. I feel like an explorer, and these future horizons are both exciting and a little daunting—precisely where they ought to be.

This book reflects the data I've collected, and some of my experiences, but you've had your own experiences as a changemaker and as an observer of other changemakers. Your insights, ideas, and the wisdom you've gained over time are all valuable, and I encourage you to find ways to activate what you've learned as you pursue your change-making path.

Finally, your active participation is essential in the journey to being a changemaker. In keeping with the spirit of this catalyst-handbook, you get the last word. While this is the book's conclusion, it's your turn to write your own introduction or, if you're already on your way, to continue writing your own next chapter.

Whatever you do, please do start somewhere, because our world needs you more than ever.

What's next for you?

What about this book resonated with you?

What simple changemaking lessons would you add?

What would you modify?

How can your notes and reflections be a map for your future?

Finally, where will you go from here? What is one small step you can start this week?

APPENDIX

NUTSHELL ANATOMY OF THE RESEARCH PROJECT

My definition of a changemaker is anyone who steps up—through paid and/or volunteer work, financial philanthropy, official mentorship, or unofficial encouragement—to make a positive change in the world. This includes their piece of the world, be it workplace, local neighbourhood, or global community.

I began my research project by emailing everyone I knew, asking for referrals to potential interviewees. My Inbox was soon flooded with suggestions of changemakers to contact.

I contacted the changemakers to schedule interviews: 30–40 minutes with a standard set of questions. Sometimes, if a changemaker had more time to offer, I asked more questions, but the core questions were consistent. I asked:

- How they went from having a good idea to taking action on it.

- What helps them keep working day after day, even when it gets hard.
- What they're most proud of.
- What obstacles get in their way (and how they overcome them).
- How they handle naysayers.
- What they'd do differently.
- What advice they have for aspiring changemakers.

Every interview with a changemaker felt like a master class in how to be a better human.

In the interest of being thorough in this, your change-maker handbook, the specific questions were:

1. Describe the difference you're making in the world/ at work/in your community.

2. Out of everything you've done to make a difference in the world/at work/in your community, what are you most proud of?

3. I use this term 'changemaker' a lot. What term(s) do you use to describe yourself? How do others describe you?

4. Lots of people have great ideas for how they want to make a difference or change the world; how did you go from having a great idea to taking action on it?

5. What motivates/inspires you to keep doing the work day after day, even when it gets crappy and hard?

6. What are the key things you've done/actions you've taken that have helped you be successful? What would you do differently?

7. What's the biggest obstacle you've faced? How did you overcome it?

8. Have you encountered naysayers? How did you handle them?

9. What would make your work even more satisfying?

10. Where do you turn when you need help (including specific people, resources, tools/structures)?

11. What piece of advice would you offer up to aspiring changemakers (about what to do or what not to do)?

I interviewed 30 women and 18 men, Canadian and US-based, who are teachers; authors; activists; volunteers; leaders in the public, non-profit, and corporate sectors; financial philanthropists; community leaders; and coaches. Forty-eight changemakers. For a list of the changemakers I interviewed, visit: www.karaexner.com

My original plan was to interview 100 people, but one of the interviewees, Dr. Riane Eisler, author, historian, scientist, and speaker, asked me to explain my project. After I did, she asked, "Do you really need 100?" I thought, wow, if Riane Eisler questions the necessity of 100, I'd better pay attention.

I typed (or handwrote for a few in-person interviews) as fast as I could while the interviewees spoke. After each interview, while the conversation was still fresh in my brain, I fixed my shorthand to ensure the written record reflected the changemakers' words accurately. (As an aside, this would be a piece of advice I would offer aspiring researchers: if you can, invest the time, money, and technology to record your interviews.)

With the help of two research assistants, I analyzed every sentence in every interview to see what themes emerged. What started as five flip chart pages on my living room floor became a lengthy word document with about 20 themes. Thanks to some specific advice from a trusted mentor ("You have too many themes of too many different types; I think they can be sorted into these three categories"), I grouped the themes thus:

- How changemakers perceive themselves
- How changemakers relate to others
- How changemakers orient themselves to action

REFERENCES

Biswas-Diener, R. (2010). *Practicing Positive Psychology Coaching: Assessment, Activities, and Strategies for Success.* John Wiley & Sons.

Biswas-Diener, R. (2012). *The Courage Quotient: How Science Can Make You Braver.* John Wiley & Sons.

Dooley, B. (2009). *Lessons by the Book: The Evolution of Purpose.* Bedo.org. Accessed from:
https://bedo.org/bitty-bits/
lessons-by-the-book-the-evolution-of-purpose

Gilbert, E. (2014, November 1). *Thought of the Day: DON'T LIVE SOMEBODY ELSE'S DREAM. Dear Ones - I found this picture today that my husband took* [Image attached] [Status update]. Facebook.
https://www.facebook.com/GilbertLiz/photos/thought-of-the-day-dont-live-somebody-elses-dreamdear-ones-i-found-this-picture-/719990104749774/

Gilbert, E. (2017, January). *Elizabeth Gilbert's 4-Question Test to Know Whom to Trust*. Oprah.com. http://www.oprah.com/inspiration/ elizabeth-gilbert-how-to-figure-out-who-to-trust

Kashdan, T., & Biswas-Diener, R. (2014). *The Upside of Your Dark Side: Why Being Your Whole Self—Not Just Your "Good" Self—Drives Success and Fulfillment*. Hudson Street Press.

Katz, P. (2013). *PAUSE – 13.14 – Are You Minding the Gaps?* https://patkatz.com/blog/overload-overwhelm/ pause-13-14-are-you-minding-the-gaps/

Right To Play. (2020, January). *About Us, Our Mission*. https://www.righttoplay.ca/en-ca/about-us/

Starfish Project. (2020, January). *Our Story, Our Mission, The Meaning Behind the Name: The Starfish Parable*. https://starfishproject.com/our-mission-3/

Tamlyn, R. (2013). *Play Your Bigger Game: 9 Minutes to Learn, a Lifetime to Live*. Hay House.

Tamlyn, R. (2018, February 15). *Spotlight: What business are you really in?* https://www.ricktamlyn.com/ spotlight-what-business-are-you-really-in/

ACKNOWLEDGEMENTS

When I became a parent, I much better understood the phrase 'It takes a village.' Working on this book has taught me that *I* take a village. It is only with the help of my village that I have gotten to the point of publishing a book. I will always be deeply grateful that so many people assisted in my efforts to follow my curiosity and achieve my goal.

I must first acknowledge the changemaker interviewees. You were generous with your time and insights when I interviewed you, and I was delighted to get your kind permission to include your wise words to help illustrate the book's themes.

I also received permission to write about and quote others I admire, and I am grateful for your generosity, too: Robert Biswas-Diener, Pat Katz, Elizabeth Gilbert, Rick Tamlyn, Ben Dooley, Martin Parnell, Riane Eisler. Thank you for allowing me to share how I've been inspired by you.

I will always remember the day I finished writing the first draft of the manuscript. I was so relieved and also aware that I had a long journey ahead. My first step was to talk to local published authors to find out how they turned the Word document on their screen into a book they could hold in their hands. My sincere thanks to all of you for telling me how you did it. I'm delighted that I'll be in a position to pay it forward, if an aspiring author asks me the same questions.

I'm so glad I got a referral to Marie Beswick-Arthur, professional editor. It took me six months to work up the courage to send my original manuscript to her. She may not know that I was terrified to send in each subsequent version of my evolving manuscript, but she does know how I feel about her: Marie, you are a skilled editor, certainly, but beyond that, I felt you totally understood me, my goals, and my project. I know you are still in my corner cheering me on.

After I had an edited version of my manuscript, I got brave enough to start working with a self-publishing company. Thank you to the team at FriesenPress. Your friendly, professional, and patient approach is much appreciated. I'm in good hands with you.

Many people have contributed their time and expertise in this multi-year journey:

- Big thanks to Wendy Fallon for spending countless hours with me in the early years of the project, and to Lori Maloney who knew I had a few interviews left to analyze and was relentless in ensuring I finished the job so I had no more excuses. Together we analyzed each sentence of every interview to organize all the changemakers' words into tangible themes.

- My thanks to Bobbi Lee for learning about the world of self-publishing and sharing with me the most important bits, and for asking the smart business questions when my brain is focused on completely different matters.

- My 'beta readers' Melissa Casey, Amy Lister, and Lori Maloney devoted significant time providing detailed feedback on an early draft, making the manuscript much better. And they are also at the top of my list whenever I need some quick advice.

- I didn't have a title for this book for the longest time, and it was becoming quite a problem. My thanks to Tony Myers for giving me a fresh perspective, and to Denise Summers (the Title Queen) for creating – in 24 minutes flat – the perfect title.

I sometimes tell the story of how I first got the idea to do an informal research project. My favourite part of the story is how my community of professional coaches offered only positive support and encouragement, even for my zany initial idea to interview 100 changemakers. Dozens of colleagues and friends locally and around the world have given me tangible help and personal encouragement to pursue writing this book. My sincere thanks to all of you for telling me over and over that I could do it.

A small handful of trusted allies has given me direct help and held me accountable to achieve this dream: Gord Aker, Diane Bonneau, Melissa Casey, Ric Durrant, Carlo Jensen, Heather Kuttai, Amy Lister, Bob Nogue, Janet Reid. You all have invested considerable time and energy to help me create better reflective questions, refine my ideas, and remember my purpose. You have seen me ugly cry, have listened patiently to my doubts, and have kicked my ass to get this project done. Thank you.

My parents, Merv and Joan, were my first changemaker role models. They were—and still are—community volunteers, and they have travelled the world making a difference. I am grateful for your early example and for your on-going cheerleading.

Thank you to my boys Solomon and Graydon. You are bright lights in my world. After fending for yourselves for so many meals and enduring my incessant talk about "the book," I suspect you will be just as happy as I when it finally gets launched. (Although you've gotten so good at cooking your own meals, I think it's best if you continue.)

To my husband, Scott: You have always treated my ideas, my goals, my projects, and my evolving priorities as if they are the most natural and expected things in the world. Thank you for always showing me confidence and trust.

ABOUT THE AUTHOR

Kara Exner holds a BA in Psychology and a Master's degree in Adult and Continuing Education. While interviewing nearly fifty successful changemakers, she heard the same themes raised over and over, and decided to document what makes changemakers universally successful. As a leadership coach, she is credentialed as a Professional Certified Coach with the International Coaching Federation, and has worked with hundreds of people to help them understand how they perceive themselves, how they relate to others, and how they can reach their goals. She lives in Calgary, Canada, with her husband and their two boys.

Printed in Canada